ALSO BY MARK STRAND

Almost Invisible

Almost Invisible

MARK STRAND

Alfred A. Knopf · New York
2012

THIS IS A BORZOI BOOK
PUBLISHED BY ALFRED A. KNOPF

Copyright © 2012 by Mark Strand
All rights reserved. Published in the United States by Alfred A. Knopf,
a division of Random House, Inc., New York, and in Canada
by Random House of Canada, Limited, Toronto.
www.aaknopf.com/poetry

Knopf, Borzoi Books, and the colophon are
registered trademarks of Random House, Inc.

Library of Congress Cataloging-in-Publication Data

Strand, Mark [date]
Almost invisible / Mark Strand.—1st ed.
p. cm.
"This is a Borzoi book."
ISBN 978-0-307-95731-3
I. Title.
PS3569.T69A79 2012
811'.54—dc22
2011025432

Jacket photograph by Vincent Laforet / *The New York Times* / Redux
Jacket design by Chip Kidd

Manufactured in the United States of America
First Edition

to MC

"Gentlemen," returned Mr. Micawber, "do with me as you will! I am a straw upon the surface of the deep, and am tossed in all directions by the elephants—I beg your pardon; I should have said the elements."

—Charles Dickens

CONTENTS

Almost Invisible

A Banker in the Brothel of Blind Women

A banker strutted into the brothel of blind women. "I am a shepherd," he announced, "and blow my shepherd's pipe as often as I can, but I have lost my flock and feel that I am at a critical point in my life." "I can tell by the way you talk," said one of the women, "that you are a banker only pretending to be a shepherd and that you want us to pity you, which we do because you have stooped so low as to try to make fools of us." "My dear," said the banker to the same woman, "I can tell that you are a rich widow looking for a little excitement and are not blind at all." "This observation suggests," said the woman, "that you may be a shepherd after all, for what kind of rich widow would find excitement being a whore only to end up with a banker?" "Exactly," said the banker.

Bury Your Face in Your Hands

Because we have crossed the river and the wind offers only a numb uncoiling of cold and we have meekly adapted, no longer expecting more than we have been given, nor wondering how it happened that we came to this place, we don't mind that nothing turned out as we thought it might. There is no way to clear the haze in which we live, no way to know that we have undergone another day. The silent snow of thought melts before it has a chance to stick. Where we are is anyone's guess. The gates to nowhere multiply and the present is so far away, so deeply far away.

Anywhere Could Be Somewhere

I might have come from the high country, or maybe the low country, I don't recall which. I might have come from the city, but what city in what country is beyond me. I might have come from the outskirts of a city from which others have come or maybe a city from which only I have come. Who's to know? Who's to decide if it rained or the sun was out? Who's to remember? They say things are happening at the border, but nobody knows which border. They talk of a hotel there, where it doesn't matter if you forgot your suitcase, another will be waiting, big enough, and just for you.

Harmony in the Boudoir

After years of marriage, he stands at the foot of the bed and tells his wife that she will never know him, that for everything he says there is more that he does not say, that behind each word he utters there is another word, and hundreds more behind that one. All those unsaid words, he says, contain his true self, which has been betrayed by the superficial self before her. "So you see," he says, kicking off his slippers, "I am more than what I have led you to believe I am." "Oh, you silly man," says his wife, "of course you are. I find that just thinking of you having so many selves receding into nothingness is very exciting. That you barely exist as you are couldn't please me more."

Clarities of the Nonexistent

To have loved the way it happens in the empty hours of late afternoon; to lean back and conceive of a journey leaving behind no trace of itself; to look out from the house and see a figure leaning forward as if into the wind although there is no wind; to see the hats of those in town, discarded in moments of passion, scattered over the ground although one cannot see the ground. All this in the vague, yellowing light that lowers itself in the hour before dark; none of it of value except for the pleasure it gives, enlarging an instant and finally making it seem as if it were true. And years later to come upon the same scene—the figure leaning into the same wind, the same hats scattered over the same ground that one cannot see.

The Minister of Culture Gets His Wish

The Minister of Culture goes home after a grueling day at the office. He lies on his bed and tries to think of nothing, but nothing happens or, more precisely, does not happen. Nothing is elsewhere doing what nothing does, which is to expand the dark. But the minister is patient, and slowly things slip away— the walls of his house, the park across the street, his friends in the next town. He believes that nothing has finally come to him and, in its absent way, is saying, "Darling, you know how much I have always wanted to please you, and now I have come. And what is more, I have come to stay."

The Old Age of Nostalgia

Those hours given over to basking in the glow of an imagined future, of being carried away in streams of promise by a love or a passion so strong that one felt altered forever and convinced that even the smallest particle of the surrounding world was charged with a purpose of impossible grandeur; ah, yes, and one would look up into the trees and be thrilled by the wind-loosened river of pale, gold foliage cascading down and by the high, melodious singing of countless birds; those moments, so many and so long ago, still come back, but briefly, like fireflies in the perfumed heat of a summer night.

Dream Testicles, Vanished Vaginas

Horace, the corpse, said, "I kept believing that tomorrow would come and I would get up, put on my socks, my boxer shorts, go to the kitchen, make myself coffee, read the paper, and call some friends. But tomorrow came and I was not in it. Instead, I found myself on a powder-blue sofa in a field of bright grass that rolled on forever." "How awful," said Mildred, who was not yet a corpse, but in close touch with Horace, "how awful to be so far away with nothing to do, and without sex to distract you. I've heard that all vaginas up there, even the most open, honest, and energetic, are shut down, and that all testicles, even the most forthright and gifted, swing dreamily among the clouds like little chandeliers."

The Students of the Ineffable

What I am about to say happened years ago. I had rented a house by the sea. Each night I sat on the porch and wished for some surge of feeling, some firelit stream of sound to lead me away from all that I had known. But one night, I climbed the hill behind the house and looked down on a small dirt road where I was surprised to see long lines of people shuffling into the distance. Their difficult breathing and their coughing were probably caused by the cloud of dust their march had created. "Who are you and why is this happening?" I asked one of them. "We are believers and must keep going," and then he added, "our work is important and concerns the self." "But all your dust is darkening the stars," I said. "Nay, nay," he said, "we are only passing through, the stars will return."

The Everyday Enchantment of Music

A rough sound was polished until it became a smoother sound, which was polished until it became music. Then the music was polished until it became the memory of a night in Venice when tears of the sea fell from the Bridge of Sighs, which in turn was polished until it ceased to be and in its place stood the empty home of a heart in trouble. Then suddenly there was sun and the music came back and traffic was moving and off in the distance, at the edge of the city, a long line of clouds appeared, and there was thunder, which, however menacing, would become music, and the memory of what happened after Venice would begin, and what happened after the home of the troubled heart broke in two would also begin.

The Buried Melancholy of the Poet

One summer when he was still young he stood at the window
and wondered where they had gone, those women who sat by
the ocean, watching, waiting for something that would never
arrive, the wind light against their skin, sending loose strands
of hair across their lips. From what season had they fallen, from
what idea of grace had they strayed? It was long since he had
seen them in their lonely splendor, heavy in their idleness, en-
acting the sad story of hope abandoned. This was the summer
he wandered out into the miraculous night, into the sea of
dark, as if for the first time, to shed his own light, but what he
shed was the dark, what he found was the night.

Ever So Many Hundred Years Hence

Down the milky corridors of fog, starless scenery, the rubble of ocean's breath, that lone figure strolling, gathering about him without shame a small flood of damages, concessions to a frailty which was his long before he knew what he must do or what he must be, and now, with his hand outstretched as if to greet the future, he comes close and pours out to me the subtlety of his meaning and I see him, my long-lost uncle, great and golden in the sudden sunlight, who predicted that he would reach over the years and be with me and that I would be waiting.

Exhaustion at Sunset

The empty heart comes home from a busy day at the office. And what is the empty heart to do but empty itself of emptiness. Sweeping out the unsweepable takes an effort of mind, the fruitless exertion of faculties already burdened. Poor empty heart, old before its time, how it struggles to do what the mind tells it to do. But the struggle comes to nothing. The empty heart cannot do what the mind commands. It sits in the dark, daydreams, and the emptiness grows.

Clear in the September Light

A man stands under a tree, looking at a small house not far away. He flaps his arms as if he were a bird, maybe signaling someone we cannot see. He could be yelling, but since we hear nothing, he probably is not. Now the wind sends a shiver through the tree and flattens the grass. The man falls to his knees and pounds the ground with his fists. A dog comes and sits beside him, and the man stands, once again flapping his arms. What he does has nothing to do with me. His desperation is not my desperation. I do not stand under trees and look at small houses. I have no dog.

You Can Always Get There from Here

A traveler returned to the country from which he had started many years before. When he stepped from the boat, he noticed how different everything was. There were once many buildings, but now there were few and each of them needed repair. In the park where he played as a child, dust-filled shafts of sunlight struck the tawny leaves of trees and withered hedges. Empty trash bags littered the grass. The air was heavy. He sat on one of the benches and explained to the woman next to him that he'd been away a long time, then asked her what season had he come back to. She replied that it was the only one left, the one they all had agreed on.

The Gallows in the Garden

In the garden of the great house they are building an immense gallows. The head of the great house, who wears a dark suit which he believes shows him to great advantage, defends the gallows' size by saying that the executed will thus appear small in death. But his critics, whose taste in clothes can never match his, say that the huge gallows will only signify the importance of the hanged. Nonsense, explains the head of the great house, the gallows are more than the gallows and the hanged are less than the hanged. Anything else is unthinkable.

Love Silhouetted by Lamplight

The arm of smoke, grown thin, reaches across the water and settles briefly on a small house near the woods. A husband and wife, each with a drink in hand, are sitting inside, arguing about which of them will die first. "I will," says the husband. "No, I will," says the wife. "Maybe we'll die at the same time," they both say in unison. They cannot believe that they are talking this way, so the wife gets up and says, "If I were an artist, I would paint a portrait of you." "And if I were an artist," says the husband, "I would do exactly the same."

The Triumph of the Infinite

I got up in the night and went to the end of the hall. Over the door in large letters it said, "This is the next life. Please come in." I opened the door. Across the room a bearded man in a pale-green suit turned to me and said, "Better get ready, we're taking the long way." "Now I'll wake up," I thought, but I was wrong. We began our journey over golden tundra and patches of ice. Then there was nothing for miles around, and all I could hear was my heart pumping and pumping so hard I thought I would die all over again.

The Mysterious Arrival of an Unusual Letter

It had been a long day at work and a long ride back to the small apartment where I lived. When I got there I flicked on the light and saw on the table an envelope with my name on it. Where was the clock? Where was the calendar? The handwriting was my father's, but he had been dead for forty years. As one might, I began to think that maybe, just maybe, he was alive, living a secret life somewhere nearby. How else to explain the envelope? To steady myself, I sat down, opened it, and pulled out the letter. "Dear Son" was the way it began. "Dear Son" and then nothing.

Poem of the Spanish Poet

In a hotel room somewhere in Iowa an American poet, tired
of his poems, tired of being an American poet, leans back in
his chair and imagines he is a Spanish poet, an old Spanish
poet, nearing the end of his life, who walks to the Guadalqui-
vir and watches the ships, gray and ghostly in the twilight,
slip downstream. The little waves, approaching the grassy bank
where he sits, whisper something he can't quite hear as they
curl and fall. Now what does the Spanish poet do? He reaches
into his pocket, pulls out a notebook, and writes:

> Black fly, black fly
> Why have you come
>
> Is it my shirt
> My new white shirt
>
> With buttons of bone
> Is it my suit
>
> My dark-blue suit
> Is it because

I lie here alone
Under a willow

Cold as stone
Black fly, black fly

How good you are
To come to me now

How good you are
To visit me here

Black fly, black fly
To wish me good-bye

The Enigma of the Infinitesimal

You've seen them at dusk, walking along the shore, seen them standing in doorways, leaning from windows, or straddling the slow-moving edge of a shadow. Lovers of the in-between, they are neither here nor there, neither in nor out. Poor souls, they are driven to experience the impossible. Even at night, they lie in bed with one eye closed and the other open, hoping to catch the last second of consciousness and the first of sleep, to inhabit that no-man's-land, that beautiful place, to behold as only a god might, the luminous conjunction of nothing and all.

A Dream of Travel

Comes down from the mountain the cream-colored horse, comes across dun fields and steps lightly into the house, and stands in the bright living room cloudlike and silent. And now, without warning, the gray arm of the wind takes him away. "I loved that horse," thought the poet. "I could have loved anything, but I loved that horse. With him I could have gone to the sea, the wrinkled, sorrowing sea, and who knows what I could have done there—turned wind into marble, made stars shiver in sunlight."

The Emergency Room at Dusk

The retired commander was upset. His room in the castle was cold, so was the room across the hall, and all the other rooms as well. He should never have bought this castle when there were so many other, cheaper, warmer castles for sale. But he liked the way this one looked—its stone turrets rising into the winter air, its main gate, even its frozen moat, on which he thought someday he might ice skate, had a silvery charm. He poured himself a brandy and lit a cigar, and tried to concentrate on other things—his many victories, the bravery of his men—but his thoughts swirled in tiny eddies, settling first here, then there, moving as the wind does from empty town to empty town.

Once Upon a Cold November Morning

I left the sunlit fields of my daily life and went down into the hollow mountain, and there I discovered, in all its chilly glory, the glass castle of my other life. I could see right through it, and beyond, but what could I do with it? It was perfect, irreducible, and worthless except for the fact that it existed.

Provisional Eternity

A man and a woman lay in bed. "Just one more time," said the man, "just one more time." "Why do you keep saying that?" said the woman. "Because I never want it to end," said the man. "What don't you want to end?" said the woman. "This," said the man, "this never wanting it to end."

The Street at the End of the World

"Haven't we been down this street before? I think we have; I think they move it every few years, but it keeps coming back with its ravens and dead branches, its crumbling curbs, its lines of people just stepping from a landscape that goes blank the moment they leave it. And what of the walled city with its circling swallows and the sun setting behind it, haven't we seen that before? And what of the ship about to set off to the isle of black rainbows, and midnight flowers, and the bearded tour guides waving us on?" "Yes, my dear, we have seen that too, but now you must hold my arm and close your eyes."

The Nietzschean Hourglass, or The Future's Misfortune

Once, as my thought was being drawn through daylight into the bronze corridors of dusk and thence into the promise of dark, I heard out there the strained voice of the hourglass calling for someone to turn it over and show that the future is just an illusion, that what lay ahead was only the past again and again. I was too young for such an idea, so it came back years later as if to prove its own point.

An Event About Which No More Need Be Said

I was riding downtown in a cab with a prince who had consented to be interviewed, but asked that I not mention him or his country by name. He explained that both exist secretly and their business is carried on in silence. He was tall, had a long nose beneath which was tucked a tiny mustache; he wore a pale-blue shirt open at the neck and cream-colored pants. "I have no hobbies," he explained. "My one interest is sex. It can be with a man or a woman, old or young, so long as it produces the desired result, which is to remind me of the odor of white truffles or the taste of candied violets in a floating island. Here, let me show you something." When I saw it, saw how big it was, and what he'd done to it, I screamed and leaped from the moving cab.

A Short Panegyric

Now that the vegetarian nightmare is over and we are back to our diet of meat and deep in the sway of our dark and beautiful habits and able to speak with calm of having survived, let the breeze of the future touch and retouch our large and hungering bodies. Let us march to market to embrace the butcher and put the year of the carrot, the month of the onion behind us, let us worship the roast or the stew that takes its place once again at the sacred center of the dining room table.

Hermetic Melancholy

Let's say that night has come and the wind has died down and the blue-green trees have turned to gray and the ice mountains, slick under the scarred face of the moon, are like ghosts, motionless in the distance, and the moon's weak light streams into the room where you sit at a table, staring into a glass of whiskey, and where you have been so long that the night, so still, so stark, has become not only your day but the whole of your life; and let's say that while you are there the sun, the actual sun, has risen, and it occurs to you that what you made of the night was only a possibility, a painless, rarified form of despair that could lead, if continued, to an unwanted conclusion, and you realize that the words you chose were not the right words—you were never the person they suggested you were; now let's say that there is a loaded gun in the house and you toy with the idea of using it and say, "Go ahead, shoot yourself," but here, too, the words are not right, so, as you have often done, you revise them before it's too late.

A Letter from Tegucigalpa

Dear Henrietta, since you were kind enough to ask why I no longer write, I shall do my best to answer you. In the old days, my thoughts like tiny sparks would flare up in the almost dark of consciousness and I would transcribe them, and page after page shone with a light that I called my own. I would sit at my desk amazed by what had just happened. And even as I watched the lights fade and my thoughts become small, meaningless memorials in the afterglow of so much promise, I was still amazed. And when they disappeared, as they inevitably did, I was ready to begin again, ready to sit in the dark for hours and wait for even a single spark, though I knew it would shed almost no light at all. What I had not realized then, but now know only too well, is that sparks carry within them the wish to be relieved of the burden of brightness. And that is why I no longer write, and why the dark is my freedom and my happiness.

Mystery and Solitude in Topeka

Afternoon darkens into evening. A man falls deeper and deeper into the slow spiral of sleep, into the drift of it, the length of it, through what feels like mist, and comes at last to an open door through which he passes without knowing why, then again without knowing why goes to a room where he sits and waits while the room seems to close around him and the dark is darker than any he has known, and he feels something forming within him without being sure what it is, its hold on him growing, as if a story were about to unfold, in which two characters, Pleasure and Pain, commit the same crime, the one that is his, that he will confess to again and again, until it means nothing.

There Was Nothing to Be Done

Sorrow was everywhere. People on street corners would suddenly weep. They could not help themselves. In dark apartments, in parked cars, at roadside tables, people wept. The dog by his master's side, the cat on the sill, they wept as well. The king and the queen had died and so had the prince, and the president of the republic, and the stars of the silver screen. The whole world wept. And the weeping went round and round and could not stop.

No Words Can Describe It

How those fires burned that are no longer, how the weather worsened, how the shadow of the seagull vanished without a trace. Was it the end of a season, the end of a life? Was it so long ago it seems it might never have been? What is it in us that lives in the past and longs for the future, or lives in the future and longs for the past? And what does it matter when light enters the room where a child sleeps and the waking mother, opening her eyes, wishes more than anything to be unwakened by what she cannot name?

In the Afterlife

She stood beside me for years, or was it a moment? I cannot remember. Maybe I loved her, maybe I didn't. There was a house, and then no house. There were trees, but none remain. When no one remembers, what is there? You, whose moments are gone, who drift like smoke in the afterlife, tell me something, tell me anything.

Futility in Key West

I was stretched out on the couch, about to doze off, when I imagined a small figure asleep on a couch identical to mine. "Wake up, little man, wake up," I cried. "The one you're waiting for is rising from the sea, wrapped in spume, and soon will come ashore. Beneath her feet the melancholy garden will turn bright green and the breezes will be light as babies' breath. Wake up, before this creature of the deep is gone and everything goes blank as sleep." How hard I try to wake the little man, how hard he sleeps. And the one who rose from the sea, her moment gone, how hard she has become—how hard those burning eyes, that burning hair.

On the Hidden Beauty of My Sickness

Whenever I thought of my sickness I would hear the melancholy sound of a viola. When I described it to the doctor, he heard the same sound. "You should keep your sickness to yourself," he said. One cloudless summer day, I went outside; some crows gathered around me and were silent. I took this as a tribute to the hidden beauty of my sickness. When I told the doctor, he said, "Your sickness may be catching and could ruin everything. Therefore, I am no longer your doctor." Yesterday, when I considered my sickness, I saw my parents, naked in the baking heat, kissing and whispering. I was worried where my sickness was leading me, and turned my attention to a distant town, to its golden clock, its white stone villas, its boulevards crowded with angels shielding their eyes from the sun.

With Only the Stars to Guide Us

Whenever the giants turned in for the night, taking their huge toys with them, we were left nothing to play with, and slept under sofas and chairs. The gift of bigness would never be ours. This was a truth against which we had tried again and again to turn our tiny backs, and each time had failed. Undone by sorrow, some of us found solace in prayer, and others, like ourselves, chose to follow wild dogs through the dark, moose-crowded woods of the northland, nursing their hurt until they dropped.

Trouble in Pocatello

It was autumn. It was late in the day. A storm was coming. Flocks of birds were flying south. A pink-and-purple sunset stained the house, the wind gusted, branches tossed, leaves dropped like dead moths on a sisal rug. "I'm home," said the husband. "Not again," said the wife.

Like a Leaf Carried Off by the Wind

After leaving work, where he is not known and where his job is a mystery even to himself, he walks down dimly lit streets and dark alleys to his room at the other end of town in the rear of a rundown apartment house. It is winter and he walks hunched over with the collar of his coat turned up. When he gets to his room, he sits at a small table and looks at the book open before him. Its pages are blank, which is why he is able to gaze at them for hours.

The Social Worker and the Monkey

Once I sat in a room with a monkey who told me he was not a monkey. I understood his anguish being trapped in a body he detested. "Sir," I said, "I think I know what you are feeling, and I would like to help you." "Treat me like a monkey," he said. "It serves me right."

Nobody Knows What Is Known

A man and a woman were on a train. The man said, "Are we going someplace? I don't think so, not this time. This is already the next century, and look where we are. Nowhere. Tell me, Gwendolyn, when we boarded the train, why hadn't we known this day would come?" "Snap out of it," Gwendolyn said. The train was crossing an endless, snow-covered plain; no town awaited its arrival, no town lamented its departure. It simply kept going, and that was its purpose—to slither dreamlike over blank stretches of country, issuing sorrowful wails that would slowly fade in the cold.

Those Little Legs and Awful Hands

Night had fallen. A man who was staying at the Grand Hotel walked to the beach, lit a cigar, opened a black umbrella, and leaned back in a canvas beach chair, holding the cigar in one hand and the umbrella in the other. I wanted to ask him, why the umbrella, but I was too timid. Then, I heard him say, "Those little legs and awful hands, will I never be rid of them?" I patted my legs, then looked at my hands, and knew that he had not meant me, and certainly not himself, but maybe another, someone he might have hated, or even loved. But down the beach, a woman, wearing very large mittens, was coming toward him, rapidly, with baby steps. He jumped up from the beach chair, tossed his cigar, and with his umbrella began to run; he ran and ran, trying to escape, as if he could ever escape.

Not to Miss the Great Thing

It was to happen. He knew it would happen. He would have secret knowledge of when that would be, and be there early to welcome it. The gates to the city were closed. A cloud lowered itself into the central square and disappeared into an unmarked alley. A large woman with sequins in her hair studied him from a distance. A cold rain fell on all the houses but his. Suddenly it stopped, and he walked out into the yellow light. Maybe it's come, he thought, maybe this is it, maybe this is all it is.

Nocturne of the Poet Who Loved the Moon

I have grown tired of the moon, tired of its look of astonish-
ment, the blue ice of its gaze, its arrivals and departures, of
the way it gathers lovers and loners under its invisible wings,
failing to distinguish between them. I have grown tired of
so much that used to entrance me, tired of watching cloud
shadows pass over sunlit grass, of seeing swans glide back and
forth across the lake, of peering into the dark, hoping to find
an image of a self as yet unborn. Let plainness enter the eye,
plainness like a table on which nothing is set, like a table that
is not yet even a table.

In the Grand Ballroom of the New Eternity

They sway like drunks in delirious exile from sense, letting their blindness guide them ever further from what might have been theirs, letting their former selves fade and be lost in the dusk of forgetfulness, never to be regained, never to be more than an idea of once having been, so that the light which had been theirs is gone for good. And when the doctors come, it is too late. The shades above the city have already been drawn, the pockets of wind have been emptied.

When I Turned a Hundred

I wanted to go on an immense journey, to travel night and day into the unknown until, forgetting my old self, I came into possession of a new self, one that I might have missed on my previous travels. But the first step was beyond me. I lay in bed, unable to move, pondering, as one does at my age, the ways of melancholy—how it seeps into the spirit, how it disincarnates the will, how it banishes the senses to the chill of twilight, how even the best and worst intentions wither in its keep. I kept staring at the ceiling, then suddenly felt a blast of cold air, and I was gone.

ACKNOWLEDGMENTS

The author gratefully acknowledges the following publications in which these poems first appeared, sometimes in slightly different form: *Boston Review, Jerusalem Review, Jubilat, Kenyon Review, Little Star, Meatpaper, New Republic, The New York Review of Books, The New Yorker, Pear Noir, Poetry, Salmagundi, Slate.*

I wish to thank Dana Prescott and the staff of Civitella Ranieri, where, as a guest, I was able to begin this book. I would like to thank Wiljan van den Akker and Esther Jansma, for their enthusiastic involvement in the ordering of the poems. I would also like to thank Deborah Garrison, my editor, for her insight and unerring advice throughout the making of this book.

A NOTE ABOUT THE AUTHOR

Mark Strand is the author of thirteen books of poems. He is also the author of a book of stories, three volumes of translations, and monographs on the artists William Bailey and Edward Hopper, and the editor of a number of anthologies. He has received many honors and awards for his poems, including a MacArthur Fellowship, the Pulitzer Prize (for *Blizzard of One*), and the Bollingen Prize. In 1990 he was appointed Poet Laureate of the United States. In 2009 he was awarded the Gold Medal for poetry from the American Academy of Arts and Letters. He teaches at Columbia University.

A NOTE ON THE TYPE

This book was set in a version of the well-known Monotype face Bembo. This letter was cut for the celebrated Venetian printer Aldus Manutius by Francesco Griffo, and first used in Pietro Cardinal Bembo's *De Aetna* of 1495.

The companion italic is an adaptation of the chancery script type designed by the calligrapher and printer Lodovico degli Arrighi.

Book design and composition by Robert C. Olsson
Printed and bound by Thomson-Shore, Dexter, Michigan